How To Manage Your Money

Getting Rid Of Debt, Loans, Credit Card Debt, And
Mortgages Is A Proven Strategy That Can Help You Take
Control Of Your Financial Freedom

*(Understanding And Effectively Managing Your Own
Finances Is The Topic Of This Article)*

Morton Adkins

TABLE OF CONTENT

You Invest To Experience Among

People sometimes go to extreme lengths in today's world merely to follow the latest trends. As long as people feel comfortable, it doesn't really matter how much it costs. This could be the precise cause of your money management difficulties. Who says you have to utilize the newest automobile, phone, watches, clothes, shoes, and everything else? According to a wise man, there is always a location to obtain goods appropriate for one's social and economic standing, no matter where they are in life.

Everything has its time. Spend within your limits; there's no need to put yourself under needless pressure to follow the trends. Today, a large number of people owe money only to feel included. Why would you borrow money for anything like a birthday celebration or to get a phone, pair of shoes, clothes, or even just to celebrate? When you spend money only to feel like you belong, you'll never succeed financially.

Spending for needs rather than wants is the way of the wise. Understanding the distinction between needs and wants will significantly alter your financial situation. Don't get me wrong; there is absolutely nothing wrong with having enough money to live within your means after reserving a portion. The trouble arises when you spend everything you own to emulate others who only own a small portion of what others own.

Let me reiterate this as a reminder: distinguish between what you need and what you want! "What you want" refers to items that you might enjoy but are not absolutely necessary; thus, you can live without them. Conversely, "what you need" refers to items that are so essential to your life that you cannot function without them.

Your financial situation is the best indicator of what you have and don't need. You won't pass away if you don't follow the trends! To eat the seed you should sow, don't follow those who are reaping the rewards of their labour.

Nobody was meant to live the same life twice. Knowing oneself and moving at your speed are prerequisites for wisdom. Make sure you stick to your present budget while making every effort to improve your financial situation.

Be aware that those who spend as much as they do today and are still financially comfortable are the ones who have consistently lived within their means up until this point. The finish line represents the destination for anyone who, via perseverance, patience, and consistency, stays in the race at all times. It's not necessarily wrong to stand out; there's no criminal in feeling apart. Stand out rather than blend in!

You're Lacking A Vision.

Even though it seems so simple, this can have been the end of your financial success. You could also ask, what is the relationship between vision and money? A great deal! Regardless of their circumstances, people stand out because of their vision.

Vision is the perception of sight through mental means. My problem is that individuals have a vision for almost everything they want to achieve or become, but they don't think having a vision is vital when it comes to saving money. Before taking a single physical step, a person with vision travels a thousand miles in their thoughts. A person with sight is capable of seeing anything because it is such a strong sense. This is as easy as seeing; your direction is determined by what you perceive. You so become stagnant if you are blind.

How does this actually affect your finances now? Having a clear vision for your goals and aspirations will naturally influence how you manage your finances. When it comes to managing your finances, vision becomes essential since it will help you stay focused, instil a sense of responsibility, provide direction, foster discipline and determination, encourage conservative spending, and accelerate your progress.

Let me briefly refresh your memory: when did you wish to purchase a phone?

Do you recall how careful you were with your money until you had the exact amount required to make the purchase? The power of vision was at work when you were able to obtain the precise amount required to buy the phone by being thorough, focused, and disciplined enough.

The benefit of the power of vision is that it can help you maintain the proper amount of money needed to carry out concrete tasks in your life. It is not limited to saving money for a phone. However, lacking vision when handling your finances may lead to financial irresponsibility, confusion, and impulsive spending. You still wonder why you spend so much money. I suppose not.

What can you see, rather than how much money you spend, should be the question at hand. Without any motivation to save, you'll always struggle to hold onto your money.

Step 5: The Most Value for Your Money Approach

We have to make sure we're obtaining the greatest deal possible on expenses like insurance, social bills, and interest debt. Our goal with the best bang-for-your-buck approach is to maintain our accounts at their optimal value.

Let's examine which categories to apply this strategy to using our budget data.

Social Bills: Internet, TV cable, cell phone, etc.

We all adore our communication and entertainment services, but are we really getting the most for our money? Combining these services can result in significant savings, but we need to compare our prices to those of other providers first.

If our charges are reasonable, we may easily request a better deal from our service provider by getting in touch with them every few years. If we've been loyal consumers, the business will probably make an effort to satisfy us. If a provider's contract binds you, this can still function.

Home, auto, health, and life insurance

Everybody needs insurance, and the cost of such policies may rack up. Insurance bundling can be beneficial.

Every year, changes in the corporate sector and our personal lives have an impact on insurance premiums. We may save hundreds of dollars by contacting our insurance company once a year to inquire about better prices.

Debts with interest: credit card debt, auto loans, financing, etc.

It may be more difficult to search for lower interest rates on debts with interest. Our credit record and DTI may have had an impact on the amount and kind of debt we had when we first applied for the loan.

We must first decide what we want from the new loan and whether our credit has improved enough to warrant it before searching for another one.

Among our debt improvement goals are High APR and Lower APR. We would like to get a lower interest rate on a debt that now has a higher-than-average rate.

From Compound to Simple Interest: We would like to obtain a loan with a simple interest rate or one with fewer compounding periods because we have debt with various compounding periods.

From several loans to one loan: We wish to combine all of our loans into a single one.

Every goal involves a savings component, but before moving further, make sure your credit report is in good order, and there aren't any excessive hard requests.

You should also think about how your available credit is doing. Our spending patterns may also influence our borrowing practices. Allowing ourselves to have more credit may only make our bad borrowing habits worse.

For instance, what should we do with the additional credit that becomes available if we combine two credit cards that are at maximum limit into one? All we have accomplished, if we use it, is a greater debt load.

It is better to think of the best bang-for-your-buck strategy as an annual task. Every year, we ought to designate a certain month to review all of our services and invoices and apply the best value for the money approach to each.

We may clear the path to a better financial future and a more contented and meaningful life by realizing the pitfalls of the rat race and acting to establish a more balanced and purpose-driven life. The following are some reasons why it's critical to identify the rat race:

Awareness: You become more conscious of the things that are keeping you back and keeping you from reaching financial freedom by realizing the rat race and its pitfalls. This can assist you in taking a more proactive and calculated approach to managing your money and assist you in avoiding the typical errors and traps that a lot of people encounter.

Motivation: Realizing that life is a rat race might inspire and motivate one to escape its entanglements and seek a more satisfying existence. You might be more inclined to take chances and try new things in order to accomplish your goals if you recognize that other routes lead to success and happiness.

Perspective: Understanding the rat race might help one understand the real worth of money and time. You could be more inclined to look for alternate sources of income or make investments in things that yield passive income if you realize the true costs of running in the rat race, such as missing out on time with friends and family or experiencing stress from never-ending job demands.

Control: You may take charge of your financial destiny and make wise decisions about your desired way of life by learning to identify the rat race and its pitfalls. You can seek a more rewarding and independent lifestyle by being more deliberate with your time and money rather than feeling trapped in a cycle of work and spending.

A change in viewpoint and knowledge of the typical patterns and behaviours that ensnare individuals in cycles of labour and consumption is necessary to identify the rat race. Here are a few indicators that you are in the rat race:

The grind from 9 to 5: A prevalent indication of the rat race is the 9–5 grind, in which individuals put in long hours at a job that provides little autonomy or fulfilment. You can be caught in the rat race if you find yourself forced into a job you don't enjoy and feel like you're only working to make ends meet.

Existing paycheck to paycheck: Living paycheck to paycheck or having little to no savings or investments is another typical indicator of being in the rat race.if you find yourself worrying about money all the time and finding it difficult to save for the future.

High costs: Those who are involved in the rat race frequently have high costs because they are trying to maintain a particular lifestyle or meet the demands of their jobs. if you find yourself spending more than you make, accruing debt, or being unable to save money.

Lack of autonomy: Being a part of the rat race frequently results in a lack of control over one's time and resources. if you are unable to explore other interests or sources of money or if you find yourself working nonstop.

Stress and burnout: People who are in the rat race may experience stress and burnout as a result of finding it difficult to balance their personal and professional lives and feeling as though they are always on a treadmill. You can be a victim of the rat race if your work or way of life is overwhelming or burning you out.

You can begin to take action to escape the rat race's entanglements and pursue a more contented and independent lifestyle by being aware of these telltale indicators.

Making Investments

Investing entails buying things that are meant to yield a profit with the hope that the investor will eventually make more money than they first invested. Risks are associated with investing, and not all investments yield a profit. This is where the correlation between risk and return is observed.

Typical investing options include stocks, art, mutual funds, real estate, and commodities.

The most significant component of personal finance is investing, which is also one of the areas where the best guidance is provided. There are big differences in risk and return between different investments, so many people are looking for help with this aspect of their financial strategy.

Defence

A variety of products are needed for personal protection in order to guard against unintentional and dangerous situations.

Typical forms of personal protection include health insurance, life insurance, and estate preparation.

This is another difficult area of personal finance where consumers typically seek professional advice. To precisely ascertain an individual's insurance and estate planning requirements, a comprehensive suite of analyses is required.

Individual Budgeting phases of management

Following a well-thought-out plan is essential to proper financial management. A budget or a planned financial plan might incorporate all of the aforementioned personal finance areas.

Typically, personal bankers and investment advisors create these plans after working with their clients to identify their goals and needs and then taking the necessary action.

Generally speaking, the primary components of the financial planning process are:

Evaluation, goal-setting, plan creation, execution, monitoring, and reevaluation

Keep in mind that creating a budget or financial plan is essential to achieving your family's and your own goals.

Every stage of your family life may present different challenges and opportunities. Planning is one of the most crucial things you can do to be ready for the next big event in your life.

Whether you are getting married or having a kid, it is crucial to be ready for the financial toll that these events will take on your life. It's crucial to be adaptable because starting a family could be one of the biggest financial decisions you make. Enhancing family budgeting can facilitate the shift and create long-term financial security.

Act As A Quality Supplier

Collectively, we accumulate value in the workplace through our labour as representatives or through the goods and services we offer for sale. It's unlikely that an amazing exhibition audit will be enough to guarantee a promotion or even to maintain your career. Furthermore, a fantastic product or service definitely won't be enough on its own.

Prioritize giving mentality

Value is determined by the observer (think about how much extra you might pay for an umbrella on a rainy day). Employees who are easy to get along with and reliable with their work will be more valuable to their manager than those who cause conflict in team meetings and routinely miss deadlines.

Additionally, a customer will find an item more beneficial if their #1 celebrity endorses it, is on sale, or includes a contribution reward. At the same time, we are growing numb to commercials; therefore, we must be cautious of follow-up offers, upsells, and other products. Today, what we value most is credibility; that's what we're after.

In light of the ongoing competition in the labour market, workers must establish their value to the company in order to be hired and retained in their roles, advance to more senior positions, and attract clients by demonstrating a visionary approach to business. Many customers are under duress and feeling agitated, so they are being cautious with their purchases. However, there is a virtual glut of discounts available right now.

Customers are choosing the products and services they believe would be most beneficial. You must increase the perceived value of what you have to offer. But you also have a responsibility to look out for your friends, family, and yourself. What, then, do you do?

services that won't break the bank but are still very beneficial, like a digital book that can be downloaded or a CD.

Make contact with someone who manages your market for free and ask them to contribute an additional commodity or service. They guarantee your customers' or clients' openness, and you receive an extra reward for your offer, so it's a win-win situation.

Increase the perceived value of your product or service by adding case studies and recommendations. Think about the people who may possess the highest level of "cultural capital" within your audience.

Usually, this will be someone your leads can relate to because they have similar struggles and circumstances OR someone they look up to because they have accomplished what they are trying to do.

Consider ways to increase the perceived value of what you offer by viewing the scenario from your client's point of view. Is there anything about your product or service that you don't think is important but that others do? If you're not sure, review satisfied customers and buyers.

Workers and business owners demonstrate your value to your team by acting as a connection. Keep an ear out for issues that individuals need and connect them with resources, persons, or services that can provide them. Do this for professional initiatives and additional office responsibilities, but also for personal problems. For instance, suggest that the two of you discuss a wonderful occasion site that someone has told you about and that they are planning for their next vacation.

Highlight the extra value you are now offering to your clientele. Maybe you keep receiving tidbits of knowledge that everyone else overlooks. Instead of assuming that your clients will notice, bring them up in an email or blog post. The cream has a chance to rise to the top in this competitive, serious commercial market and challenging economy. Make sure you assist others in seeing your value and the reasons you are the best in the business.

Chapter 2: Preserving

Everyone should emphasize saving since it's a crucial component of personal finance. Putting money down for a rainy day, a major purchase, or retirement can provide you with financial stability and peace of mind.

Savings Account Types

Traditional savings accounts, money market accounts, and high-yield savings accounts are among the several kinds of savings accounts that are accessible. It's critical to conduct due diligence and select the best account type for your needs, as each has pros and cons of its own.

The most prevalent kind of savings account is the traditional savings account. Banks and credit unions provide them, and their interest rates are usually lower than those of other account kinds. With no minimum balance requirements and user-friendly online banking capabilities, they are also incredibly accessible.

Savings accounts and money market accounts are comparable, although money market accounts often provide greater interest rates. They may have stricter withdrawal limits and a larger minimum balance requirement, but they're still a decent choice for those looking to increase the interest on their savings.

however, the former can have even greater interest rates. Internet banks usually provide them and may come with certain restrictions, like a lack of physical branches or poor customer support.

Making a Plan for Savings

Making a savings strategy comes next after opening a savings account. This entails determining how much you must save each month to meet your savings target and defining a savings goal.

Establishing your savings target is the first stage in developing a savings strategy. This might be anything from setting up a savings account for a down payment on a home to creating an emergency fund. You can calculate how much you need to save each month to attain your goal once you've determined what it is.

For instance, you would need to save $416.67 every month to reach your goal of saving $10,000 in two years.

It's crucial to create an achievable and realistic savings plan. Do not give up if you are unable to save the amount you had hoped to. Simply modify your strategy and continue pursuing your objective.

Putting money aside for emergencies

Having cash on hand for emergencies is one of the main motivations for saving. This could involve unforeseen costs for things like auto maintenance or hospital visits.

This can provide you with a safety net and keep you out of debt in the event of unforeseen expenses.

As you begin to accumulate emergency savings, figure out how much you need to live on each month. Next, increase that figure by three or six to get the amount you want to save. To find out how much you need to save each month, divide that amount by the total number of months you have to save.

Retirement Savings

In order to prepare for retirement, saving is also quite crucial. It's crucial to save extra money on your own, even if your work offers a retirement plan.

It's crucial to conduct a study and select the best alternative for you because each of these has pros and cons of its own. Employers provide 401(k) plans, which let you fund your retirement accounts with a part of your pre-tax salary. A matching contribution is something that many businesses offer as well, which can help you save even more.

You can save money on your own through individual retirement accounts (IRAs) and Roth IRAs.

But what if the reverse is true—that is, the smallest loans do not have high-interest rates?

Here, the circumstances are different, and given that the entire process is centred around a feeling of achievement and the psychological component of the principle at play, it might make more sense to pay off your debts at higher interest rates overall before paying off your low-interest debts. Depending on your financial circumstances, this could result in you paying less interest over time.

Financial analyst Frankel notes that there might be some variations in the situations in which this approach is appropriate and that he frequently disagrees with the typical snowball strategy in one particular area.

"Even though the Snowball method suggests it should be done, it will be a bad idea to process the repayment of the car loan first if someone has debts of a $15,000 credit card with a 20% interest rate and a $14,000 car loan balance of 4%."

Frankel emphasizes the importance of examining the financial situation and examining it further to determine what would happen in the event of a "snowball" effect or to prioritize repayment from the outset. After all, the longer it takes to pay off debt, the higher the interest rates.

This implies that not everyone is able to pay off their obligations using the snowball method.

So, who is not supposed to use the snowball method?

Financial expert Frankel responds, "Snowball method is likely to be a bad option for someone with a credit card debt greater than the balance of a loan." This means that people whose large debts have higher interest rates than their low-interest debts should not use it.

What happens when the loan is paid off, and how can you avoid taking on further debt and stay debt-free?

Time said, "It is unrealistic to expect a straightforward and easy way to get rid of debt, and emergency expenses can cut your progress easily."

Here, however, it's preferable to pick up where you left off, take a deep breath, and start restoring a strategy right away. But spare yourself the agony of debt once more.

The best course of action is to pay off the smallest debt first and then restart using the snowball method, but the most crucial thing is to persevere and not give up.

It is crucial to stay out of the situations that come with being debt-free once your debts are paid off, such as Refraining from using the lack of debt as justification to begin living a lavish lifestyle.

Frankel advises keeping the same amount of money you would have used to pay off the debt, but instead of using it to pay off loans or credit card payments, put it into investments or savings. By doing this, you'll learn to be frugal with your expenditures and have a better financial future.

Procedures for Recovery from Default

As soon as you discover that your loan has defaulted, you must contact your guarantee agency right once to arrange for payment. You probably won't be able to pay off the whole loan amount at once, depending on how much is owed. As a result, you'll probably need to arrange a payment schedule.

To get your debt out of default and create a payment schedule, follow these steps:

1. Request a payment schedule by giving your guarantee agency a call.

2. Give the customer support representative as much information as you can on your financial situation so that you can establish a payment schedule on an income-based default rehabilitation plan that you can afford.

3. Find out how long it will take to consolidate your debt, receive new

loans, and have the default note removed from your credit report.

4. Select a payment method, such as direct debit or automated payments from your bank or savings account, to guarantee that payments are made on time every month.

5. After your payments are completed, confirm with your guarantee agency that a request to have the default removed from your records has been submitted to all three credit agencies (Equifax, TransUnion, and Experian). Even though the late payments will still be shown, it won't appear as though you aren't making your loan payments.

6. Order free credit reports from all three bureaus at

www.annualcreditreport.com to confirm that the default has been erased from your credit report.

Even while it could be tempting to merge your loans right away, hold off on pressing the Enter or pen keys until you've read the following text.

Exercise caution

You won't get rid of your federal student loan default on your credit record unless you complete the full default rehabilitation process. Otherwise, your default normally stays on your credit report for seven years.

According to Holler, combining your federal debts after three on-time payments helps you avoid most ramifications, such as wage garnishment and an inability to receive new student loans if you return to school. But your loan will still be reported on your credit report as delinquent for seven years! Making just six more on-time monthly payments puts your federal debt eligible for rehabilitation. At this point, your loan will be reissued by the Department of Education, or if an FFELP loan is eligible to be sold by your guarantor to a new lender, you can establish a new payment term.

Once a new lender purchases your rehabilitated loan, the guarantor instructs the national credit bureaus and your original lender to remove the derogatory credit marks previously reported, and you can start with a relatively clean slate. Although you may still see missing payments on your credit report, your account won't be damaged by the student loan equivalent of a car repossession or a foreclosed home.

And remember that those payments, nine months in total, are set based on your financial situation.

The standard is uniform across all services. Income-based repayment will now be part of the equation, so you could theoretically have a payment of $5 and still get out of default. Never give up hope. Most student loan situations are manageable with the knowledge to make good choices.

Developing A Budgeting Strategy That Suits Your Needs

One of the first steps toward financial stability is making a budget. It can assist you in monitoring your spending and locating places where you can make savings. In this chapter, we'll go through the actions you may take to make a budget that suits your needs.

Ascertain Your Revenue and Outlays

such as your rental income, salary, and any additional sources of money. Next, compile a list of every expense you incur, such as rent or mortgage, utilities, groceries, entertainment, travel, and other costs.

Sort Through Your Bills

After you've made a list of every expense you incur, divide it up into fixed and variable costs. Fixed expenses are those that don't change every month, including your insurance, car payment, and rent or mortgage. Monthly expenses like groceries, utilities, and entertainment are examples of variable expenses.

Establish Financial Objectives

Establish financial goals once your income and spending have been ascertained. This could be anything from debt repayment to vacation savings. Ensure that your objectives are time-bound, meaningful, quantifiable, achievable, and specific (SMART). You may maintain your motivation and attention on your budgeting plan by setting financial goals.

Make a Plan for Your Budget

Make a financial plan with the data you have acquired. Deduct your expenses from your revenue first. If you have extra cash, think about putting it in a savings account or toward your financial objectives. Find strategies to reduce your expenses if you're spending more than you're making. Reducing your amount of eating out, cancelling unused memberships, or looking for ways to save money on utilities are a few examples of how to do this.

Monitor Your Expenses

Keep tabs on your expenditures to ensure that you are adhering to your budget. You can use an app for budgeting or keeping track of your receipts. Regularly review your spending to find areas where you're going over budget, then make the necessary adjustments to your budget.

Advice and techniques:

When establishing financial goals, use common sense. Setting and achieving objectives that are both difficult enough to keep you motivated is crucial.

Look for ways to save costs on regular purchases, such as purchasing generic brands or using coupons.

Think about automating your savings by establishing recurring deposits into a savings account.

Although it can be difficult, developing a budget is a crucial first step toward financial stability. You may take charge of your finances and work toward reaching your goals by figuring out your income and expenses, making a budget, and setting financial objectives. To stay on track, don't forget to keep an eye on your expenditure and adapt as necessary.

Comprehending Danger and Return

When attempting to increase their money through astute investing, financial backers should keep two things in mind: risk and return.trade-off between these two components in investments.

Risk refers to the susceptibility of an investment. It's the possibility that you won't make the expected returns or that you might even lose all or part of your initial investment. Different investments carry different levels of risk. Investing in equities, for instance, typically carries greater risk than keeping your money in a savings account. On the other hand, bonds are in the middle.

On the other hand, return is the asset or advantage you hope to obtain from your investments. It's the additional funds you obtain over your initial investment. Returns can take many different forms, including interest, earnings, and capital growth. Generally speaking, you should expect a more notable potential return the bigger the risk you're ready to take.

One way to think of the trade-off between risk and return on investments is as a teeter-totter. You should accept a greater degree of risk if you hope to increase your return. On the other hand, you might have to consent to lower profits if you prioritize well-being and detest risk.

A few key points to keep in mind when evaluating the risk-return trade-off are as follows:

1. The act of diversification Investing in a variety of resource classes, such as stocks, bonds, real estate, and so forth, can help reduce risk and maintain possible returns.

2. Time Skyline: The timeline of your investments plays a crucial part. If your goal is long-term, you may be able to tolerate higher levels of risk in your portfolio since you have the time and energy to ride out market fluctuations.

3. Risk Resilience: Assess how comfortable you are with danger. Some people are able to handle periods of market promise and disappointment, while others prefer more stability. Your financial goals and your level of risk aversion should be compatible.

4. Investment Information: Become knowledgeable about the various options for investments that are available. With the right information,

you can effectively manage risk and make well-informed decisions.

5. Speak with a Financial Advisor: In the unlikely event that you are unsure of how to strike a balance between risk and return, tailor an investment process to your specific needs and goals.

Talking about financial behaviour is an uncommon method that helps people express themselves more honestly and often significantly reduces the discomfort associated with financial behaviour. 3. Determine who you are financially.

Your financial identity is shaped by your attitudes, convictions, emotions, behaviours, and financial relationships.

You may identify early warning indicators of resistance to financial change and handle the uncertainty that will inevitably surface as your financial status improves by having a clear grasp of your financial identity. List all the components of your financial identity as you currently perceive them in your prosperity diary, allowing room for adjustments in the future.

Observing the repeated "I" statements you make, like "I'll never make enough money," will reveal a lot about your financial status.

4. Make Just One Modification outside of the body. By purposefully altering a minor behaviour and paying attention to your inner responses, you might learn to

adapt to new financial behaviours. Here are a few possible results:

Place your toothbrush in a different location.

• Select a new street to go to a location you frequently visit.

• Lie in bed a little later or rise earlier than normal.

• Switch the news channel.

• Invest in a magazine that you haven't previously seen.

• Replace one serve of ice cream or cake with a healthy snack.

• Go to the meeting you've been thinking about attending.

• Invert the toilet paper roll in your restroom. Practice the new action until you are comfortable doing it. Watch out for any signs of disorientation and how long it takes you to become used to the overall change.

Some people feel pain for a few days, while others could endure it for several weeks.

Once you have established your pace and started more new habits, you will be able to predict fairly accurately how long the risks and moving stupids will endure. 5. Modify One Financial Practice. Take a look at your financial management practices to get ready for financial progress. Here are a few possible results:

• Maintain a continuous tabulation of your daily income and expenses.

• Make on-time weekly bill payments.

• Quit using the credit card that you prefer. Save the cash you would have spent, even if it's only $3 a week.

• Give out some small cash.

• Spend a day living frugally.

When you make this modification, be mindful of your feelings and record them in your prosperity journal. For the time being, note down any discomfort you are feeling.

6. Keep an eye out for any resistance to changing your finances.

If you had trouble completing the previous step, consider the following:

• Will my self-perception change if my financial status changes?

• If I am financially successful, what will I worry will happen? Will my identity change if I have financial security? Will my interactions with my family change as a result? Would wealth entail the betrayal of a friend or perhaps a member of one's family?

7. Make a statement

To get the intended effects, the subconscious mind adopts and uses these ideas. If you tell your subconscious mind that life is full of opportunity, it will bring opportunities to you; if you tell it that you never get what you want, it will do the opposite.

On the other hand, conflicting beliefs and resistance to change can result in disruption.

For example, it makes no difference how often I tell my subconscious mind that I have an easy cash flow if I also believe, in opposition to that, that it is hard for me to make money.

The same goes for any pain, even dread, that I might experience as a result of easy financial flow.

Chapter 2: The Finest Methods for Creating a Budget ■◆

Overview

For some people, starting college could seem like an exciting prospect. Others, nevertheless, find it a frightening task for many reasons. Enrolling in a university or college after high school graduation is a big step. Many children often experience their first taste of independence from the outside world and leave the safety and security of their homes.

For the students' college to be successful, a number of elements must be balanced. College students have many things to think about, from studying and attending classes to handling and networking finances. One is to use caution when spending money.

Techniques for Managing Money.

The majority of students do not manage their money well. People frequently spend money without considering their budget or the consequences of making large purchases. Here are some strategies you might want to think about if you want to budget your money wisely while you're studying:

• Sign up for meal plans.

Meal plan subscriptions are one approach to saving costs. A pre-paid program is called a meal plan. This is when, each semester, you pay a certain amount of money for your meals on campus. Furthermore, meal planning is practical. You don't have to make your lunch or snack; you can choose when you want to eat it.

• Split Bills with Your Roommate.

If you want to save money on your study expenses, you could also consider dividing costs with a roommate. You should anticipate sharing a small space with other students if you live in a dorm.

It's possible to split several expenses with your roommate. Furniture and food are a couple of them.

• Be cautious while making rash purchases.

It could be tempting to spend money on things you enjoy but don't need. You must adjust your spending because you will need money for other essentials like clothing and schooling.

Books and supplies. Check your expenses instead of buying these things with your money. Next, apply this to the people in your life that you actually depend on the most.

Organizing your finances is one of the easiest aspects of your life to change. It's fundamental to take control of the money that enters and leaves your household. Many people acknowledge that not having money makes their life more complicated and stressful, but what if you weren't keeping your finances organized, so they worked as hard as they could for you? Let's look at some ways you can take control of your finances to make your life easier.

Describe Your Financial Principles and Set Objectives

Setting the right goals might be aided by understanding what matters most to you when it comes to money. No matter how "fantasy" your goals seem at the moment, establishing them and then working to create a plan to get there can make things easier.

Once more, where you are in the survey It's not necessary to cause chaos in order to streamline and smooth things out. Proceed with your entire financial life and discover your current situation. What commitments do you have, how much do you spend, how much money do you bring in, and how much have you saved? When you go through this, try not to judge yourself; just write everything down.

Maintain Fewer Accounts

Now that you know what you have, let's assume that you have a few records that need to be checked and saved. Other than wanting to distribute the money due to bank protection, there aren't many reasons to keep a ton of records. Nevertheless, if you're like the great majority, you can get by with only one bank account and one set of financial records. In the unlikely event that you own your own company and require a distinct record for business purposes, that is a unique situation. Fewer records imply less effort spent monitoring them and less benefit for thieves.

Eliminate Paper

Being paperless is something that many offices are happy about these days, and you can do the same at home. All of your bills should be configured for paperless charge, which means they will arrive in your inbox by email. That's the alternative. If your bank offers bill payment options, they usually also provide e-billing options, which you can easily set up online in a few clicks.

Give up using credit cards.

If you have many Visas, put all but one of them on hold for a moment. Make use of the card that has no fees and the lowest loan amount possible, and pay it off each time you receive a statement. Alternatively, use the card that has the greatest mobility focus to receive free travel when paying bills solely. The truth is that you should choose one and use it exclusively.

Handle Your Debt as a Consumer

If you are currently communicating customer obligation adjustments on rotating credit accounts, learn how to handle them quickly. Taking care of them on one card, if you can get them to stick together, will make things much easier.

Invest in Funds Rather than Individual Stocks

Investing in individual equities is a research and resource-intensive process. By reserving resources, you can simplify things and save time. For example, if 2045 is when you plan to step down, they might be referred to as "the 2045 asset". Given the asset's longer lifespan, the stock fraction of the asset automatically adjusts to help you avoid risk.

Spend Money More Frequently

When you go out, use cash to pay for items rather than credit or debit cards. Having cash on hand makes it easier to stick to a budget because you won't have to worry about losing track of receipts, card numbers, or records.

Give Up Services You're Not Needing

Examine any scheduled payments that appear in your records. Think about whether you really need them or not. Is it reasonable to assume that you are interacting with them as you thought you might? When did you most recently use it? For example, you may be surprised to learn that you seldom ever use your HBO GO account now that Game of Thrones is over. Those little dollars can pile up.

Your Indebtedness

Let's look at your debts after addressing your savings, spending, and mindset. If you are heavily indebted, you may assume there is no way out and even wish to avoid thinking about the subject at all. Alternatively, you may have given up on ever being debt-free and come to terms with the fact that you and our society as a whole will always have outstanding liabilities.

You should know that you are not alone if any of those things apply to you. More importantly, though, I plan to refute these assumptions in the section that follows.

Let us begin by discussing why debt feels so commonplace in today's world. Generally speaking, there are two reasons why we take on debt and spend money before we have it. First off, some purchases are so costly—take a house, for instance—that it is almost never possible to save up the entire amount of money before making the purchase. Or if you did, you might not be able to purchase your first home until you're fifty or sixty years old!

The second reason is less rational and more related to our incapacity to restrain our desires: we want the newest technology, a larger vehicle, or a trip to a far-off place. And now, not tomorrow is when we want them all. Because we've grown so used to wanting more, we no longer care as much about the financial consequences of fulfilling our desires right away. This is partly because we see people around us enjoying things that we also desire and partly because we may feel that we deserve or earned those things.

stressing over how you're going to pay those debts back later—along with all the additional interest and potential personal strain that goes along with it. Well, that's just a fact of life.

Debt and making purchases before having the money to pay for them appear to have taken precedence in the lives of many individuals and even in society at large. We consider being in debt to be the norm. But just because someone else has debt doesn't mean that's the best course of action. Due to the necessity of making payments to your creditors, having debt is expensive and stressful and may force you to work at a job you dislike.

If you could save up for such purchases before making them, wouldn't it be much less stressful, more fulfilling, healthier, and affordable? Just picture yourself feeling empowered by the knowledge that you were able to save and prepare ahead for anything. That would truly be a worthy endeavour! (You may choose to leave out long-term investments in assets, such as the property I previously mentioned, or start a business, which can be too costly to pay for with cash up front.)

I want you to start today with a very important goal: to pay off all of your debt. Does it seem like a mountain too big to climb? Keep in mind that you will always be paying interest and compound interest on your loans, which can result in a very costly and drawn-out payback cycle. You won't have to waste money on loans for items you might have bought months or years ago once you are debt-free. Paying for past expenditures will take up a significant portion of your cash flow once you pay off your final obligation, leaving you with more money to establish a stable financial future. You don't have to worry about how you're going to pay the bills that are past due and stashed in a shoebox under the bed.

Lastly, you have a higher chance of qualifying for a loan and may even be able to obtain one with better terms if you ever need one, say for a large purchase like a house. Your chances of being able to repay your mortgage and your bank's perception of you as less of a risk increase when you demonstrate your ability to manage money (e.g., by having few outstanding debts). As a result, the bank is more likely to approve your mortgage application and offer you a reduced interest rate.

Make It Memorable And Distinct.

Keep in mind that consumers prefer customized products, and the more distinctive, the better. Successful salespeople understand that building rapport with the customer initially is beneficial because it allows them to emotionally connect with the product, which helps to seal the transaction and forge future commercial relationships. Similarly, an internet marketer needs to show his actual self by convincing the customer that he needs the goods being given. It is just not possible to hide behind your website's pages and expect purchases to follow. Businesses that are successful at selling online show a human touch in a number of ways, such as social media, where customers may engage with your brand and get a sense that you appreciate and care about their satisfaction.

Okay, to help clarify, let me give you a few instances.

Create an auto-responder so businesses may customize emails and social media posts. Always address a prospective customer by their first name, personalize the email to make him feel special, and make it seem as though it was written only for him.

Furthermore, a money-back promise that is personally backed by the seller's name and even a picture can be an incredibly effective instrument for fostering confidence and easing customer regret. Customers want to know that you stand behind the goods you sell and that they are interacting with a real person rather than an automated robot.

One of the best ways to showcase the human side of your business is through social media and blogging. Consumers will always value communication with the seller, both before and following the transaction, as it gives them peace of mind that they won't be left in the dark if they have questions or need assistance at any moment.

Successful internet shops nowadays provide easily upgraded 24/7 support services for their customers. A large number of online shoppers shop late at night, well after physical stores have closed for the evening, or even from a different time zone than the vendor.

especially when combined with gift or coupon codes. The survey's findings also offer useful market research, enabling businesses to better tailor their products to the shifting demands of the consumer base. It will be much simpler to target particular individuals as a result.

Having products in every price range is crucial, Additionally, there are situations when a consumer just wants to try out your product before buying a more expensive item, so offering a free trial or demonstrating the value you offer might help. Keep in mind that some customers don't have a lot of money to spend right now. By providing lower-priced things, you can get your consumers interested by letting them sample the product and the company's very valuable customer service. Data indicates that a significant number of these low-cost clients will eventually upgrade and remain with the business provided they are happy with the service and product they have received from you.

Thus, never forget that providing excellent customer service should come first.

Okay, to summarize, consider emails that you look forward to receiving. Do you anticipate receiving emails from a specific company? Why, if so? Are there any business-related lessons you could use on your own? It's possible that you eagerly await information from your favourite social media influencer. In any case, while creating your email campaign, consider your preferences as a client and make an effort to put yourself in their position. This is crucial.

Your current objective is to provide content that will make your readers want to get your next email and wonder themselves, "Will I read this again?" after they open it for the first time.

And never forget that building a long-term relationship is what keeps customers coming back for more.

How crucial is it to incorporate healthy habits and exercise?

I promise you that making exercise and good habits a part of your everyday routine is a lifesaver and the foundation of a happy, fulfilled life. Your metabolism is accelerated, your energy levels are raised, and restorative sleep is encouraged, giving you a strong start to the day. Consistent sleep patterns, careful eating, and staying hydrated are examples of healthy behaviours that are combined with exercise. By nourishing your body and mind, these techniques maximize your resilience and general performance. Exercise, whether it be a brisk stroll, a yoga class, or a morning run, revitalizes and sets the stage for a better, more balanced existence. When you incorporate regular exercise and healthy behaviours into your routine, you give yourself the priceless gifts of longevity and vigour.

Using Mindfulness to Improve Clarity and Focus

By engaging in mindfulness practices, we may sharpen our focus and observe the world with unprecedented clarity. It entails accepting our ideas and feelings without passing judgment on them, as well as being totally present and available in the here and now. We wouldn't want to be discovered behaving like a sopped chicken, would we? We learn to detach from the worries, anxieties, and diversions that frequently obscure our vision by practising paying attention to the thing we are fixated on right now. By encouraging us to approach every work and encounter with intention, mindfulness helps us give our actions meaning and complexity. We develop heightened awareness as we practice this skill (or habit), which teaches us to listen intently, observe, and reply intelligently. In the end, mindfulness is the compass that helps us find our way through the maze of our thoughts and point us in the direction of a more serene, ordered, and concentrated mind.

- How to use mindfulness exercises to improve clarity and focus

To start practising mindfulness for clarity and attention, locate a peaceful, comfortable area where you won't be bothered. Shut your eyes and inhale deeply many times, letting your body and mind unwind. Now, gradually turn your attention to your breathing. Pay attention to the sensation of the breath coming into and going out of your nostrils, as well as the rise and fall of your belly and chest. Acknowledge thoughts and distractions without passing judgment on them when they occur, and then gently bring your focus back to your breathing. Give your senses their complete attention and take in the sights, sounds, and scents around you. As you continue to practice on a regular basis, incorporate this awareness into your everyday activities, such as taking the time to fully engage in conversations, savour meals, or feel the water when taking a shower. With regular practice, mindfulness improves your capacity for concentration, leading to increased mental clarity and attention in all facets of your life.

Having an optimistic outlook for the day

A happy mood at the beginning of the day creates the foundation for a successful and meaningful day. It's similar to donning glasses that block out the bad and give you a more positive perspective on the world. Focusing on the positive, achievable, and uplifting aspects of life is a deliberate choice that goes into developing a positive view. It entails approaching every day with thankfulness, appreciating the chances it presents, and viewing obstacles as opportunities for personal development. This way of thinking empowers us to see ourselves as successful, project positivity, and radiate excitement, all of which draw good energy and motivate people around us. A positive outlook means accepting life's complexity with hope, fortitude, and the conviction that we can make every day significant and joyful rather than rejecting it.

Furthermore, having a happy outlook influences our relationships and experiences all day long. It's contagious; it makes the world a happier place by enhancing our relationships with one another. Not only can a smile, a kind word, or an encouraging gesture make us feel better, but they can also make someone else's day better. When we start the day with a good outlook, we inspire and motivate both ourselves and everyone we come into contact with.

Advice Nos. 36–40

36-Debt Repayment Plan

Eliminating debt must be one of the primary objectives. You must decide which debt to settle first and use the money to gradually move on to the next. Prepare a duplicate of the debts and determine if you wish to settle the lowest-interest bills or the highest-interest obligations first. Either approach is acceptable and will yield benefits.

37- Use a Will to Take Care of Things

If your goal is financial freedom, you should think about what would happen to your plans in the event that you die. This is particularly valid if you have kids or a family that you will be leaving behind. Give your will some thought to ensure that your intentions will be carried out and that your loved ones are taken care of.

38. The Influence of Knowledge

Learning is a continuous process. There will never be a day when you think you've arrived. You have to stay up to date on your education if you want to stay on top of the latest technologies and trends. Reading books, blogs, quarterlies, and magazines can be one way to do this. Make it a point to read or listen to something uplifting at all times.

39. Always assess your current situation and future goals.

Once a plan is finished, you should reflect on the process of getting there. Consider what you would do differently to accomplish the goal. Go forward and take lessons from your mistakes. Try to think of more creative approaches to accomplish your objectives by drawing on your prior experiences as a useful roadmap for achieving more.

40. Discover How to Be Content Where You Are While Aiming Higher

The path to financial independence is only one aspect of the larger adventure that is life. Never claim that achieving your financial objectives is the only way to happiness. When you pay off your bills, learn how to be content. Discover ways to enjoy the procedure. You have the daily choice to choose happiness, so make that choice.

7. Steer clear of debt as much as you can those expenses constantly seem to nag you. Your income may occasionally be cut in half by debt accumulation even before you take out a single dollar. Thus, try to stay out of debt as much as you can and only take out loans in times of dire need to get out of debt.

8. Avoid becoming rich quick schemes. Get-rich-quick schemes that masquerade as high-yield investment packages have cost a lot of people a great deal of

money. They give you the impression that taking a chance is necessary to make your money work for you. However, in the end, it leaves some people rich and others impoverished.

Investing is an excellent way to increase your wealth. However, not all of us are experts in investments. In actuality, most people find it easier to make money than to invest it wisely. But if executed properly, the investment might bring in a surprising windfall.

The most astute investors never put money into something they don't fully comprehend. That's

assuming a measured risk. They don't make emotional investments. In addition to other information, they rely on market forecasts and assessments and speak with experts in the industry they want to invest in. Perhaps you will also begin honing your investment skills in a desired industry. Recall that everything that seems too wonderful to be true is probably not. This rule applies to everything. Preserving your money is a better option than throwing it away on a scheme to become wealthy quickly.

Become acquainted with prosperous individuals.

"You are the product of the five individuals you spend most of your time with," it has been said. List your friends and divide them into two groups: harmful and non-toxic.

You'll realize that some of the people you hang out with are no longer worthy of your attention. Perhaps each time you go out with them, you come home emotionally spent or are coerced into drinking more than you would like to. Maybe all your friends do is spend money on frivolous items, and you've started to follow suit. Break free from these friends. You are likely to pick up on the reckless spending habits of those you spend a lot of time with. Spend time with those who are more frugal.

In summary, the financial habits you develop when you earn a little money will carry over to when you start making more. If you spend little and buy on impulse, you won't change overnight when you start making more money. If you don't budget your money a little, you'll also tend to earn more. Develop your financial intelligence by starting now. Enhance and hone your skills to increase your earning potential. You will make your future self proud.

Spending on Social Issues:

These days, drinking alcohol is actually rather common, and it's even more commonly thought of as a weekly tradition where loved ones gather together to celebrate each other's lives and share food and drink and laugh. There are currently two ways to complete this custom: either you go out to a bar where everything costs anywhere from ten to multiple times more than what it would have cost if you had stayed at home, or you buy drinks and set up a party at your place or someone else's. Although I understand that you are paying for the experience, I don't think you should have to spend several times as much for the experience as you would for the basic need that is being met.

I can support my argument with additional data by assuming that you enjoy drinking Jim Beam bourbon. A container's cost is around

₹1200 will provide 25-30ml stakes (assuming you don't spill it during the peg-making process).

Now, this single bet would cost roughly ₹250 at any decent bar. If you were to purchase 25 stakes of a similar kind, you would have to pay 25 * 250 = ₹6250, which is

5.2 times the amount you were paying for the primary option. Furthermore, we all understand that a Jim Beam would cost more in the range of ₹300 to ₹350 rather than ₹250 for a single stake.

Assuming you go out twice a month, you should be able to save up to ₹1000. However, I have used a very reasonable estimate and have not included the money you would spend on food and drinks while out. Most of us would agree that asking to be let in is far less expensive than going out. Consequently, if we include that amount in the discussion as well, we would be looking at a difference of over 300 to 400%, which is almost screaming to be spent maybe twice a month, maybe more frequently, maybe routinely.

Treat your partner properly if you really must take her to an ostentatious café; spending money on braver meetings is a better option. These interactions will live on in both your and your partner's memories. For my part, I have never truly appreciated expensive dates, but that's a tale for another time.

I'm not really an expert on relationships or a lover, but the least I can say is that your partner should be able to understand your financial situation and base their assumptions accordingly. If you feel like it's getting out of hand, that's a great time to end it.

I apologize for bringing up the racket in the previous debate, but my friends pointed out that it makes sense, considering the times we live in. They currently believe that this truth should be shown in black and white.

The total amount of money you spend on your kids or younger relatives is another thing to be angry about or mindful of. If we look at the spending patterns of people under the age of twenty, there will be a clear difference in the kinds of products and methods that these people spend their money. I'm talking about the top 5% of earners (about ₹6 lakh annually). My father's partner launched a restaurant in 2016, and ever since I've been observing these kids greedily draining their parents' bank accounts. Many of these people are regular customers of the restaurant, coming in two or three times a week to spend between ₹ 10 and ₹12 thousand. A typical request on a table is several burgers paired with a few shakes, with a normal ticket size of approximately ₹800 to 1000.

Now, some analysts may argue that this example size is insignificant. Still, given the number of restaurants operating in the Delhi NCR (National Capital Region) alone, given the costs mentioned above, and considering the kind of money these individuals make, it is safe to say that

our country is headed for financial and
health disaster.

A Guide To Personal Finances: Budgeting And Management

2.1 What Leads to Financial Difficulties?

What other example could be more fitting? The state in which the world is currently living.The epidemic of coronaviruses. By the end of 2019, Covid-19 had taken the world by storm. Brick-and-mortar establishments closed, industry stagnated, management was in disarray, and job losses began.

What the pandemic has shown us about Charles Darwin's Theory of Evolution is what we were taught in school: "Survival of the Fittest."

The people who were financially successful or had several sources of income were the ones who mentally survived. Others even started tiny businesses to make a living.

2.1.1 Misappropriation of Cash.

Not only is it a chore to earn money, but it's also an art to manage the money that comes into your bank. If you want your business to survive forever or if you want to live the best life possible with the money you have in place, the first thing you should be learning about is managing your funds, according to the U.S. Small Business Administration. book keeping and have a basic knowledge of business finances."

Managing your finances simply entails making the proper choices. When and where to spend money. Not at all! We merely want you to become wiser; we have never asked you to be a miser. Look at what can jeopardize your ability to maintain your financial security. It all comes down to the financial decisions you make.

The Final Points

Desires versus Needs

One of the famous Rolling Stones songs from the 1960s, "You Can't Always Get What You Want," touches on a problem that a lot of us deal with on a daily basis. You might not be able to obtain what you desire, but if you put in the effort, you will eventually have what you require.

How do you discern between needs and wants, and why do you have needs? For several individuals, understanding where to draw the line can make the difference between creating a profitable budget and going broke. What, then, is the difference? The majority of needs are ordinary and don't require special expenses. They include food, which leads to shopping expenditures, and heaters, which need payment for rent or a mortgage. While there are many more non-negotiable and basic items, there are also many non-negotiable items that offer flexibility.

For example, if you require a vehicle for work, you may purchase a new BMW or a used Kia sedan. The Beemer is guaranteed to amaze your friends and provide a fine driving experience, plus the price difference is significant. What is the issue that you can afford? If your annual income is $500,000, you may be able to afford the BMW without going over your budget. However, it might be wiser to stick with the Kia if you're spending $40,000 on a house.

The same rule applies to homes: should you buy a $400,000 home or rent a one-bedroom apartment? Once more, both provide ĕhelter, but at significantly different costs.

Additionally, there's the distinction between necessities and things you could live without. Consider taking a vacation to Thailand or spending a week going to state parks close to your house. Both can provide relaxing and soothing spaces for you to spend time in, but their prices are significantly different. Additionally, consider impulse buying. Imagine visiting a home improvement store to get grass fertilizer and leaving with a lawnmower that you had not intended to purchase. You might require a new mover, but before making a deposit, it's a good idea to research models and rates.

You can set aside money for certain impulse buys or product purchases, but be mindful of what you're doing, be cautious, and always ensure that your budget balances.

Seasonal Variabilities

You should expect a significant portion of your money to go toward one or more of the expenses that come up throughout the year. Holiday presents, birthday celebrations, summer vacation expenses, and back-to-school spending are a few examples. Some domain experts are for stand-alone systems, such as publishers, while others are for fundamentals. For this reason, heating your house is necessary during the colder months, and in the summer, a greater water bill may correspond with mowing your grass. Swimming suits are used in the summer and heavy jackets in the winter, making them seasonally appropriate clothing.

When creating a budget, review your results from the previous year or two, calculate the effect of yearly expenses, and then incorporate those expenses into your plan. If summer costs are significantly higher than springtime costs, make sure you save enough money in the spring to cover summertime expenses.

Examining Your Budget

Spending plans are living records. As life is constantly changing, so too do the demands on your budget. For that reason, it's wise to regularly review and adjust your budget to account for variations in income and expenses.

What are your thoughts? Adjustments should be made to your income if you get a windfall, such as an inheritance or a raise. In the event that you lose your job or take a new one, you must adjust. Marriage or divorce requires a significant adjustment of your budget. Thus, having a child does. Sometimes, the changes are more minor or transitory; for example, a medical insurance copayment may call for a short-term adjustment.

It's not necessary to completely revamp your budget when things change. Your monthly car payment is a fixed amount that is unlikely to fluctuate, much like your rent. However, other things are more negotiable. If your income declines, you may have to eat out less. If it works out, you could make a necessary purchase, save more money, or pay off debt sooner.

There isn't a hard-and-fast rule on reviewing your budget. A few financial consultants advise doing it on a regular basis. Some suggest every several months. Consider reviewing your budget when life-changing events happen and setting out time intervals to adjust for lesser items like inflation and changes in fixed costs.

Predicted and Autonomously Saved Percentages

You really ought to think about allocating a portion of your budget for automated savings. What does "automatic" mean? It's the amount of money you set aside to finance an emergency fund, pay for Christmas gifts later in the year, or establish a college fund for your children.

The best way to handle automatic savings accounts is by withholding payments. If your company offers a 401(k) plan and you are saving for retirement, sign up and have money deducted from your paycheck. A lot of employers also provide medical and childcare savings plans, which are typically tax-exempt. Additionally, you have the option to have your salary automatically transferred into a checking account and then move a portion.

Numerous strategies exist for automating savings. Speak with a financial advisor to find out more about your options and how much savings you can afford. Continue with a plan once you've simplified it. Amounts will differ, but if your employer matches contributions to your 401(k), be sure you have at least the maximum amount that will match. Your income and expenses will largely determine any further savings. Make sure you pay the rent if you have to withhold 20% of your paycheck. Knowing how much money you need and setting aside for it will ensure that you can pay your bills and get ready for the future.

Financial experts have recommended spending percentages to assist individuals who are budgeting for the first time. For example, it's recommended that you, whether you own or rent, spend no more than 30% of your gross monthly income on housing.

Smartphones are the next significant expense for consumers and likely the most temptation to overspend. particularly if financial emergencies arise.

Independent Income

Free pay denotes having a job, receiving government assistance, or having other sources of regular income that don't require you to labour (exchange your labour for money). Monthly government-backed retirement benefits are paid out if you are eligible. If you have built your business to the point where you are able to step back from day-to-day management, you will get payments regardless of the amount of time you invest. Even though the property board often mandates property care and risks resulting in one or more occupant instalments, owners of investment properties only receive a monthly leasing instalment.

You are financially free if your independent wage is adequate to cover your necessities and daily expenses.

Lots of Resources

Resources that aid in promoting independence from the rat race frequently recall investments in insurance policies, money in ledgers, and valuable property. You must first invest resources for a considerable amount of time, usually a large sum of money over an extended period, in order to use a resource while becoming independent from the rat race. For example, most financial planners will inform you that regular contributions to a 401(K) are essential to your long-term financial security and stability. For some people, this may be true if they start managing their money early (in their 20s, 30s, or even 40s). Nevertheless, those who put off starting a comprehensive financial strategy until their 50s or beyond will require enough time to fully capitalize on the power of self-multiplying dividends. Usually, their commitments don't even double when they consider growing.

It is not uncommon for problems to arise while using resources to build independence from the rat race. Think of it as a challenging exercise. By using this method to cover your daily expenses and requirements, you wish to provide a means of having enough cash on hand to pay your bills. If you are unable to sell a resource (land, for example) fast enough to release the funds prior to the anticipated date on your bill, then inconveniences may arise. People in these situations can be referred to as "cash unfortunate moguls." Their assets might be valued at over $1 million, but they can't access that value fast enough to put it to use.

Running out of resources to turn into cash before you pass away is another, potentially more problematic, issue. Essentially, you won't have any money left over to pay your payments if you exhaust all of your resources far too rapidly.

The majority of financially independent households combine the two strategies. They may receive free compensation from government-managed retirement plans, from businesses they have invested in, or from profit-paying protections; however, they also likely have accumulated a sufficient amount of assets in the real estate and securities markets to provide them with financial security, understanding they have a lot to return to if fundamental.

Life Objectives

Put in your desired payment amount in cash (resources and pay) for the lifestyle you require. Include the year in which your goals must be completed, as well as whether or not you should pay for them. Then, set up monetary mileposts at regular intervals and count backwards to your current age. These can include certain monetary amounts saved or resources acquired.

Budgetary plan

Creating and adhering to a monthly family spending plan is an important way to guarantee that all payments are paid on time and that savings and free pay are maintained. Regularly planning your finances helps you stay in control of your spending rather than giving in to the need to overspend. It also clarifies your goals. There are risks associated with charge cards and high-interest payday loans that can prevent you from building long-term financial stability. To get further guidance on the most effective way to implement the budget, review the five basic general rules that need to be followed.

Invest Time and Pay Off Debts

Understudy loans, contracts, and comparable credit are generally less dangerous with your money because they have interest rates that are far lower than those of Visas and store cards. Using charge cards, you run the risk of accruing enormous amounts of costly premium debt. Freedom is exactly the opposite of being suffocating underwater for an extended period. Obligation implies loyalty and even slavery, both of which are detrimental to the prospect of breaking free from the never-ending rat race.

Conserve

Prioritize paying yourself. That's what financial experts typically recommend. Enrol in the retirement plan offered by your employer and take full advantage of any matching commitment benefits. Having a computerized shop from your employer into a hidden stash (or a robotized move from your insurer) that can be accessed for unforeseen consumption is also an amazing plan. Additionally, take into account making an automated commitment to a financier for an IRA.

In any event, recall that the proposed amount to save is extensively addressed, and the rationality of such an asset is once in a while even referenced to given specific situations.

Contribute

There is not a lot superior and not any more reliable strategy for building your money than financial planning. Whether you pick a 401(k) or an IRA, this is the ideal moment to investigate as needs be and conclude which track you will commence. In any case, begin! That is the major phase.

Screen Your Credit

An individual's credit report impacts any financing cost connected with vehicle, truck, or home advances or renegotiates, as well as Mastercards and store cards. It, in like manner, influences irrelevant things, for example, vehicle insurance and life coverage payments. The thought process is that anyone wild in their monetary arrangements could likewise be imprudent in different everyday concerns, like driving and consuming. Collectively, people with lower FICO scores get into additional mishaps and submit bigger cases to their insurance agency than people with higher credit scores. This doesn't mean somebody with unfortunate credit is a terrible driver; a 23, similar to a male-year-old and not wedded, is not an unfortunate driver.

Nonetheless, he will pay higher month-to-month charges since he is youthful, single, and male. Unfortunately, credit is only one of many gambling pools insurance agencies use when deciding your month-to-month expenses.

Five stages for independence from the rat race

Who wants independence from the rat race? Envision this: never work a normal 9-to-6 task to procure a check and accommodate yourself and your loved ones. You'll go through your days zeroing in on what you truly love to do.

In opposition to what many might think, this attitude isn't held for more established Filipinos entering their brilliant years. Age doesn't characterize independence from the rat race; your investment funds and pay do. Furthermore, the way to independence from the rat race can be accomplished at whatever stage in life following these means.

1)Build your pay

To start with, your payment will be generally restricted to your check. Like all individuals encountering long periods of monetary freedom, you should exchange time for cash as your starting cooperation with the economy. In any case, this isn't restricted to your work. It could likewise be your side hustles utilizing the exchange you learn at your specific employment for additional monetary advantages.

The objective, then, is to make it to the point of having the option to start saving. You'll normally just get by at the outset, yet as you move up the stepping stool and progress in your vocation, your monetary premium will increment - empowering you to construct a propensity for saving.

2)Get in the clear financially by keeping away from more obligation

On the off chance that you have no obligations, attempt to keep it that way.Nonetheless, suppose that you need credit for you to purchase a house or a vehicle for your loved ones. This is reasonable and, for some individuals, even unavoidable. What you can do is attempt to take care of your obligations straightaway and try not to get into more superfluous obligations. A couple of successful ways of doing this include:

Covering your Visa adjusts if you can't bear the cost of a thing or help without a charge card and it's anything but a crisis, don't get it. If you have any desire to stay away from the enticement, don't matter for a Visa by any stretch of the imagination.

Living inside your means: prioritize your requirements before your needs. On the off chance that you get an increase in salary at work, don't blame it on expanding your optional spending.

Keeping a severe financial plan Is OK too, at times, to spend on superfluous items, yet restricting the sum you spend permits you to save more cash for crises. Life is frequently loaded up with unforeseen occasions (exorbitant vehicle repairs, clinical costs, and so on), and you need to be financially arranged when these occur - rather than venturing into the red since you don't have crisis reserves. Take care of every one of your obligations before money management. Obligations from banks and credit organizations gather revenue. It's smarter to pay them shortly when they become considerably more hard to pay off.

3)Build your investment funds and just-in-case account

Before you begin effective financial planning, it's energetically suggested you construct a just-in-case account. A backup stash is significant in case you become jobless and end up struggling to secure another position. It's additionally useful if one of your kinds of revenue falls through and your absolute pay isn't sufficient to finance your family's costs.

We prescribe saving something like three to a half years of your month-to-month expenses. What you are doing is putting resources into your inner harmony. Put this cash in an investment account and don't contact it except when crises emerge. This asset ought to keep you and your family above water while giving you sufficient opportunity to track down one more kind of revenue.

4)Begin to contribute

Whenever you have gotten your backup stash and constructed sufficient capital, you feel happy with putting resources into it; you can take a gander at all the conceivable speculation devices on the lookout. What you contribute relies upon factors like how large your capital is, your gamble resistance, and whether you favour long haul or transient speculations. Your choices can incorporate (yet aren't restricted to):

-Stocks

-Depository Bonds

-Unit Investment Trust Funds

-Common Funds

-Time Deposits

-Investment Properties

Preferably, you ought to expand your speculation portfolio. No type of venture is 100% ensured, so plunging into various kinds of speculations can assist with balancing the misfortunes on the off chance that one of your different speculations fails to work out.

5)Grow your venture past your pay

Whenever you've dug into different ventures, you'll need to keep developing your portfolio until you arrive at the point where your speculations drive more pay than your genuine compensation. This could require years, particularly if you've settled on OK low-reward ventures. In any case, if you have the persistence or the gambling capacity to bear high-risk, high-reward, long-haul speculations, you could be developing your pay at a much quicker pace.

Whenever you've arrived where your speculations drive more pay than your normal employment, and you've saved a huge sum in reserve funds, you can, at last, resign and go through your days living life to the fullest.

The automated revenue you get from your ventures ought to be all that anyone could need to keep you and your family monetarily secure.

At the point when you don't have to work for cash any longer, you'll realize you've come to independence from the rat race. Invest your energy in developing your inclinations, making every moment count, investing time with family, and living every day without limit. Whether you get to do that in your late thirties or your later years relies heavily on how far you're willing to go to contribute and accomplish monetary autonomy.

Estimate A Budget

This will assist you in figuring out how to allocate your money so that it includes your debt repayment strategy. You should be able to determine how much you spend over the same period and what.

This document will also assist you in communicating with your creditors to request an extension of the debt repayment period.

You will need to seek the services of debt experts and financial advisers as they have the essential function of advising you to this effect. Among the items on your budget list should be:

1. Monthly earnings

2. Essential outlay

3. The monthly excess

4. Determine reasonable offers.

5. List all the advantages you've had.

6. Credits for taxes

7. Retirement Plans

8. Upkeep

Once you have a payment plan in place, you need to calculate all of this information and deliver it to your creditors. This will demonstrate improved planning and tenacity in your efforts to settle your debts, and it will persuade them to give you enough time.

When creating a personal budget, start with the debts that are most important in terms of approaching deadlines or past due amounts. You will have to choose what will have to wait while you try to make ends meet, survive, and pay off your debts when you see that there is no money left over after the budget sheet is completed.

PART 5: REDUCING EXPENSES

You can track how much money you spend and where it all goes by creating a budget. With the help of your budget, you will be able to determine what areas of your life you should cut back on or give up entirely in order to make sure you can pay off your debts and maintain your standard of living while still buying necessities.

Choosing less expensive goods that are nonetheless of a high calibre means you are reducing your expenses. By doing this, you will be able to spend less money on the things you require for day-to-day living.

During this phase, your lifestyle may be completely overhauled, possibly including reducing the amount of transportation you use. If you drive a fuel-guzzler, for example, you may choose to sell it and use the proceeds to settle your bills. If you truly need a car, you can purchase an affordable model that will save you money on gas and upkeep. If you live close to your place of employment, you may choose to forgo owning a car altogether and instead choose to walk or take public transportation, depending on how close your destination is.

You can also choose more affordable electricity sources by going fully green and using solar power, or you can use energy-saving lightbulbs that lower the amount of electricity used. Similarly, you can replace your energy-hungry refrigerator with a lighter, more energy-efficient one that uses a lot less electricity.

Wholesale prices are less expensive and spare you the stress of rushing to make a loan payment when you're truly tight for cash.

When making a purchase, you have the option to haggle over the cost of certain items. While some businessmen are always looking to turn a profit, they are able to deviate when they recognise that consumers can negotiate prices. Therefore, it is not a terrible idea to try your luck and see how much the price can drop to get that necessary item.

To avoid going over your budget, you can choose to cut back on the quantity of meals from enough to just enough. Rather than having a family that gets sick a lot because of the unhealthy foods they eat, you may limit your family to only eating less expensive, healthier foods that will ensure a healthier lifestyle.

The Business Use of Emotional Intelligence Concept.

Developing a set of guidelines for effectively managing how you handle money and any other kind of riches in your life is necessary to have emotional intelligence for success in the business world. A particular perspective on the role that money should play in your life is necessary to cultivate the right mindset.

Because they take particular stances when it comes to managing their riches, the majority of wealthy people worldwide share a remarkably similar mentality. They maintain a particular level of wealth that makes them happy, and they are able to do this because they have tight daily routines. Since repetition is the mother of excellence, adhering to the idea of repetition is crucial to leading a wealthy lifestyle. You will continue to follow certain money management guidelines once you've adopted them because doing so will ensure your financial success.

It's crucial to keep in mind that in the world of finance, it's more vital to focus on staying in a position than on how you got there. Since most individuals only concentrate on what must be done to get there in the first place, this is a common premise for every kind of success.

Every year, a number of people become millionaires in the United States alone, but this does not guarantee that they will always be wealthy. Even while the number of millionaires has increased in tandem with the past ten years, bankruptcy cases have been steadily rising.

Believing in yourself and identifying your life's passions are the cornerstones of cultivating the right mindset to manage your finances. Anything that occurs in your life is important and should not be undervalued because it will ultimately lead to financial independence. If you have an interest that you find yourself engaging in more than employment, you might want to think about turning it into a way to make money. Remember that this is the largest error you can make, so don't undervalue yourself. Since you are unique, try not to spend too much time comparing yourself to other individuals.

It is feasible to possess anything unique in this world, similar to your fingerprints. Suppose playing chess is your pastime, and it consumes a lot of your time. In that case, you might choose to participate in international tournaments either online or by travelling to the locations where the events are conducted.

If you're so excellent, you'll draw attention to yourself, making it simple for you to locate competitions and other forms of funding where you can indulge your passion. It is worth noting that a number of young people nowadays make their livelihood only by playing video games, an unthinkable prospect just a few years ago.

Several nerds get together at gaming conferences these days, not just for enjoyment but also for financial gain. Consider the 2017 Rio de Janeiro, Brazil, gaming conference, which drew players from all around the globe and was well-received by fans of computer and video games. You may feel discouraged about being innovative and finding alternative sources of income if you come from a traditional home and your parents have always been anxious to make sure you land a traditional job. After all, the success your parents have attained is a result of these conventional methods.

You will need to think creatively and delve into your inner self if you want to develop a mindset for financial success. You'll come to understand that you possess an abundance of energy, and if you direct it in the proper direction, the money will begin to pursue you rather than the other way around.

The most essential component of success in the modern world is having a positive and unconventional way of thinking. Consider any billionaire in the world as an example, and consider some of the strategies they employed to achieve wealth—they merely applied creative thinking.

Chapter 5: Rapid Income Growth

We are all aware that unexpected events might occur in life and that our normal income may not be sufficient to meet all of our needs. But do not worry! In this chapter, we'll look at quick and efficient strategies to increase your revenue.

Consider it like enhancing your financial engine with a turbocharger.

Examining Prospects for Temporary Income

Okay, let's explore the realm of opportunities for temporary income. Numerous opportunities for rapid and flexible income have arisen as a result of the gig economy. Whether you're an experienced professional, a freelancer, or just someone with a strong work ethic, there's probably a platform out there that may benefit from your skills.

Determine Your Ability and Capabilities

Make sure you are aware of your abilities and skills first. Do you have an aptitude for writing, graphic design, coding, or simply simple errand running? In the gig economy, there's probably a market for whatever it is.

Examine Freelance Websites

Freelancers and clients looking for particular services are connected by platforms such as TaskRabbit, Fiverr, and Upwork. Establish a profile that highlights your abilities and begin placing bids on pertinent jobs. It's an easy method to get money for your talents.

Benefit from Short-Term Initiatives

Seek out short-term jobs or projects that fit your expertise. These can increase your income without requiring a long-term commitment and frequently have fast turnaround times.

Making the Most of Current Revenue Sources

Making the most of what you already have can sometimes be the fastest path to increasing your revenue. Let's look at some methods for making the most of your current revenue streams.

Discuss a Short-Term Pay Increase

If you work, you should think about discussing a brief pay raise with your employer. Emphasise your value to the business and describe the financial difficulties you're having. In hard circumstances, some employers could be willing to lend a hand.

Utilise Long-Term Opportunities

Make the most of overtime chances if your employer provides them. Putting in more hours, accepting more responsibility, or volunteering for unique projects are all ways to boost your income by working overtime.

Recognising Gig or Freelance Work

Gig and freelance labour have grown to be essential components of the contemporary workforce. Let's look at how you might take advantage of these chances to increase your revenue rapidly.

Examine Internet Resources

Numerous websites link clients and independent contractors. Examples include Freelancer, Guru, and Upwork. Make a strong profile, highlight your abilities, and place bids on projects that interest you.

Establish Profiles Wisely

Be thoughtful when creating a profile on a freelance network. Emphasise your best qualities, include examples of your prior work if you can, and make it obvious what makes you unique from the competition. Clients frequently use these profiles to make snap decisions.

Safe Short-Term Initiatives

Concentrate on short-term tasks that complement your knowledge and expertise. These initiatives can provide a rapid infusion of funds and frequently have quicker response times.

How to Negotiate a Bonus or Salary Increase

Although it may sound scary, negotiating a bonus or pay increase can have a radical impact on your financial circumstances. Let's look at some useful advice for contacting your boss in this chat.

Emphasise the Contributions You Have Made

Be sure to emphasise your value to the organisation when asking for a bonus or pay increase. Talk about specific accomplishments, well-executed initiatives, or any new duties you've taken on.

Demonstrate Market Analysis

Investigate wage trends in the area and your industry. This information can be a very useful negotiation tool. Your case for a rise is strengthened if you can show that your present pay is less than the industry average.

Be Open and Honest About Your Predicament

When talking about a pay increase or bonus, be open and honest about your financial status. Describe the difficulties you're having and how having more money would be very beneficial. When employers are aware of the circumstances, they are frequently more understanding.

Techniques for Rapidly Increasing Income

After looking at a number of methods for rapidly increasing your income, let's combine them all into a thorough plan.

Evaluate Your Ability and Choices

To begin, evaluate your abilities, inclinations, and accessibility. What do you enjoy doing, and what are your strengths? This will direct your search for chances to generate short-term cash.

Examine Internet Resources

Make use of web resources that link independent contractors with clients. Create thoughtfully constructed profiles, submit bids for pertinent tasks, and use your abilities to land temporary jobs.

Effective Communication

A wage increase or bonus negotiation requires good communication. Emphasise your contributions, present your market analysis, and be open and honest about your financial status.

Put Short-Term Profits First

Prioritise changes that can yield rapid profits in the near future. short-term projects, gig labour, and negotiating immediate salary increases should come first.

Maintain Balance with Long-Term Objectives

Don't let your short-term earning chances distract you from your long-term objectives. This is a tactical boost to get past short-term obstacles, but you must keep things in balance so that they fit into your larger financial plan.

In summary

Increasing your income rapidly is similar to injecting some adrenaline into your finances. It calls for some hustle, ingenuity, and skilful communication.

Never forget that you have useful abilities and that there are possibilities out there just for you.

Thus, approach it with confidence, whether you're looking at short-term assignments, negotiating a temporary pay rise, or venturing into the realm of freelancing. You're taking control of your financial future by doing more than just raising your salary. Cheers to immediate success and better financial times ahead!

The Financial Security Journey

You must set out on the Journey to Financial Security in order to attain stability and financial peace of mind. Here is a little peek at this adventure:

These objectives can include debt repayment, property ownership, emergency savings, or retirement planning.

2. Budget Creation: One of the first things to do is to create a reasonable budget. To make sure that spending is in line with financial objectives, it entails tracking income and costs. A budget offers a financial decision-making road map.

3. Emergency Fund: It's important to set up an emergency fund. This safety net keeps your financial security intact while helping to pay for unforeseen costs like medical bills or auto repairs.

4. Debt Management: One important first step is to address high-interest debt. Debt repayment, including credit card and loan repayment, eases financial strain and releases funds for investing and saving.

5. Saving and Investing: To ensure long-term financial security, one must save regularly and make prudent investments. Retirement accounts, equities, bonds, and real estate are examples of investments.

6. Retirement Planning: One of the most important parts of the journey is making retirement plans. Estimating retirement costs, funding retirement accounts, and deciding when and how to retire are all part of it.

7. Insurance Coverage: It's imperative to safeguard your assets with insurance, including life, health, and property insurance. It protects your financial security in the event of unforeseen circumstances.

8. Constant Learning: Maintaining financial literacy requires constant effort. Making educated selections is aided by knowledge of financial trends, tax planning, and investment techniques.

9. Adjusting to Life's Changes: Because life is ever-changing, flexibility is necessary for financial security. Part of the process is preparing for things like changing jobs, expanding families, and economic downturns.

10. Legacy Planning: Making sure their assets assist charitable causes or future generations is what some people mean when they talk about legacy planning. It's about making an impression that lasts.

11. Financial Peace of Mind: Getting financial security eventually results in mental tranquillity. It entails having faith in your ability to overcome obstacles related to money and accomplish your objectives.

Every person's journey is different based on their circumstances and ambitions. Along the way, it calls for perseverance, self-control, and dedication to make wise financial decisions.